THE WORDS OF
ALBERT SCHWEITZER

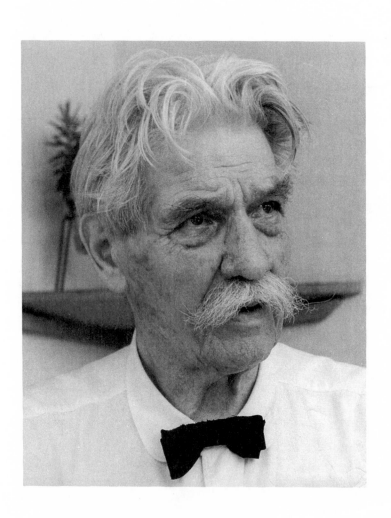

C1

THE WORDS OF
ALBERT SCHWEITZER

SELECTED BY
NORMAN COUSINS

Newmarket Press
New York

The Newmarket *Words Of* Series

This book published simultaneously in the United States of America
and in Canada.

2 3 4 5 6 7 8 9 F/C

Library of Congress Cataloging in Publication Data
Schweitzer, Albert, 1875–1965.
   The words of Albert Schweitzer.
   Bibliography: p.
   Summary: Quotations from Schweitzer's speeches and
writings on reverence for life, faith, music,
civilization, peace, and other topics.
   1. Schweitzer, Albert, 1875–1965—Quotations.
[1. Schweitzer, Albert, 1875–1965—Quotations.
2. Quotations] I. Cousins, Norman.   II. Title.
CT1018   1984   083'.1   84-18890
ISBN 0-937858-41-2

Manufactured in the United States of America

Other volumes in the Newmarket *Words* series include:
   The Words of Desmond Tutu
   The Words of Gandhi
   The Words of Martin Luther King, Jr.
   The Words of Peace: Selections from the Speeches
    of the Winners of the Nobel Peace Prize

Quantity Purchases

*Companies, professional groups, clubs, and other organizations may qualify for special
terms when ordering quantities of this title. For information, write the Special Sales
Department, Newmarket Press, 18 East 48th Street, New York, New York 10017, or phone
(212) 832-3575.*

CONTENTS

5

Editor's Note: I am grateful to Esther Margolis, of Newmarket Press, for the invitation to compile this book, and to Thurston Moore for first suggesting to her the idea for a book of Schweitzer's words. I also wish to acknowledge that Jean Anderson did more than to assist in this effort. She was the senior partner in this literary enterprise. By all rights, her part in this book deserves to be featured in every way.

INTRODUCTION
by Norman Cousins

An entire generation has come of age since the death of Albert Schweitzer in 1965. Abundant biographical materials are available for those who wish to pursue an interest in a man who won distinction in the fields of theology, philosophy, medicine, and music and, most of all perhaps, as one of the moral giants of the twentieth century. Yet nothing is more characteristic of our age than its separation from history and from those who made it. This little book, therefore, is a reminder that not so long ago there was a man whose life and work lit up the lives of people on every continent.

The basic facts about the life of Schweitzer are readily recounted. He was born on January 14, 1875, in the Alsace, a territory that alternately came under French and German sovereignty and therefore combined the cultures of both countries. Very early in life his interests in music, religion, and science forecast his various careers. His university studies led to a post as minister of a small church in Strasbourg, after which he became principal of a school of theology in that city. His writings on religion and, in particular, on the origins of Christianity attracted wide attention. At the same time, his interpretation of the life and music of Johann Sebastian Bach and his expertise as organ-builder and organist made him one of the leading musical figures of his time.

Despite this dual success, he decided to "make

my life my argument." His ideas in theology and his emphasis on personal commitment were somewhat at variance with the prevailing views. Rather than enter into debate or even dialogue, he decided to test his ideas as living reality. He returned to the university to study medicine, received his degree, and took off for Africa to found a hospital in a small village in what was then French Equatorial Africa.

For more than fifty years the Hospital of Albert Schweitzer in Lambaréné, in the Gabon, became something of a contemporary shrine. The hospital itself was rather crude, measured by modern standards of facilities and equipment. But the presence of Albert Schweitzer and his symbolic power in the modern world attracted a large number of doctors and nurses and other volunteers, who joined *Le Grand Docteur* in treating many thousands of Africans.

The basic philosophy behind the hospital must be taken into account in any evaluation of its performance. Schweitzer did not set out to build a gleaming modern hospital in the middle of the African jungle. Instead, he duplicated an African village to which he attached a clinic for dispensing medical services. Schweitzer realized that he had to meet Africans on their own terms. He knew that the sense of family was very strong among Africans and that they would not be inclined to come to a hospital in which the sick members would be separated from their immediate relatives. What he did, therefore, was to examine the ill Africans, prescribe for them, and assign them to small huts similar to those in which they lived. The family members would help care for the ill ones, according to the instructions of the hospital staff.

Other modern hospitals existed in Africa, but none attracted more patients than the Schweitzer Hospital Lambaréné. Despite the absence of modern plumbing and other conventional aspects of modern sanitation, the recovery rate at the Schweitzer Hospital compared favorably with hospitals in the Western world. Schweitzer was far ahead of his time, recognizing that the confidence of the patients in their doctors and in themselves were important factors in the healing process.

Here I borrow from a memoir I wrote about Dr. Schweitzer following my first visit to his hospital in 1957. The biggest impression of Schweitzer that emerged for me was that of a man who had learned to use himself fully. Much of the ache and brooding unhappiness in modern life is the result of the difficulty people experience in using themselves fully. We perform compartmentalized tasks in a compartmentalized world. We are reined in—physically, socially, spiritually. Only rarely do we have a sense of fulfilling ourselves through total contact with total challenge. We find it difficult to make real connections even with those who are nearest to us. But we live with vast yearnings demanding air and release. These yearnings have to do with our capacity for moral response. And our potentialities in this direction are deep—potentialities that keep nagging at our inner selves. Schweitzer had never been a stranger to his potentiality.

This is not to say that Schweitzer sought or achieved "happiness" in pursuit of that potentiality. He was less concerned with happiness than with purpose.

What was it that had to be done? How did a person go about developing an awareness of important needs? How did someone recognize a moral summons?

A full life thus defined, however, is not without fatigue. Albert Schweitzer was supposed to be severe in his demands on those who worked alongside him. Yet the demands he made on others were less than those he made on himself. He was not concerned about the attainability of perfection; what concerned him was the pursuit of perfection. When he sat down to play the piano or the organ, he might practice a single phrase for hours. But the difference between the phrase when he first played it and when he himself was satisfied with it might have been imperceptible even to a trained musical ear. He had the sternest ideas, for example, about how Bach ought to be played, and he stretched his own capacity to its fullest in his interpretations. This was no mere obsession. He sought his outermost limits as a natural part of purposeful living. If he seemed to push and prod others, it was almost an automatic carryover from his own work habits.

The main point about Schweitzer is that he brought the kind of spirit to Africa that black persons hardly knew existed in the white man. Before Schweitzer, white skin meant beatings, gunpoint rule, and the imposition of slavery on human flesh. If Schweitzer had done nothing in his life other than to accept the pain of these people as his own, he would have achieved moral eminence. His place in history will rest on something more substantial than the extent to which the floors of his hospital were swept. It will rest on the spotless nature of his vision and the clean sweep of his nobility.

The greatness of Schweitzer rests not just on what he has done but on what others have done because of him. What has come out of his life and thought is the kind of inspiration that can animate an age. He represents enduring proof that we need not torment ourselves about the nature of human purpose. His main achievement is a simple one. He has been willing to make an ultimate sacrifice for a moral principle. Because he has been able to make the supreme identification with other human beings, he has exerted a greater force than millions of armed men on the march.

KNOWLEDGE AND DISCOVERY

"Discoveries in the natural sciences that enable mankind to dispose of increasingly powerful and varied forms of energy . . . these are the most striking discoveries of our times.

"Less spectacular the discoveries in the realm of thought. Nevertheless, they are important. For there is progress to be made here, also, of which humanity has need. Through the ideas men have discovered and to which they have given their allegiance mankind has lifted itself from a primitive mentality to a state of civilization; because of the ideas conceived and circulated generation after generation civilization endures, progresses, and deepens."

"The ideas which determine our character and life are implanted in mysterious fashion. When we are leaving childhood behind us, they begin to shoot out. When we are seized by youth's enthusiasm for the good and the true, they burst into flower, and the fruit begins to set. In the development which follows the one really important thing is—how much there still remains of the fruit, the buds of which were put out in its springtime by the tree of our life."

"There is a disposition to think that because I am so deeply concerned with the need for reverence for life that my philosophy must be Buddhist, especially in connection with the Buddhist emphasis on the importance of animal life. But there is much more to Buddhism than that; and I hope there may be more to my own philosophy than that."

"Hegel has exercised strong influence on my own thought. A man of reason. But also a man with a deep respect for the possibilities of the human being, especially the capacity to embrace important new concepts. Hegel is a philosopher who attaches value to the mind concerned with the problems of its own growth."

"One would think that Descartes lived just to emit a line of staggering profundity: 'I think, therefore I am.' . . . I find it difficult to be impressed by 'I think, therefore I am.' One might as well say, 'I have a toothache, therefore I exist.' These catchwords are tricky things. I don't think they serve the cause of creative thought in philosophy."

"One can't expect philosophers to be romanticists, but it is important to remember that the philosopher must deal not only with the techniques of reason or with matter and space and stars, but with people. After all, it is the relationship of man to the universe, and not solely the relationship of one galaxy to another, or one fact to another, that should occupy such an important part of the philosopher's quest. There is such a thing as being too detached."

"The great secret of success is to go through life as a man who never gets used up."

"I wanted to be a doctor that I might be able to work without having to talk. For years I had been giving myself out in words . . . this new form of activity I could not represent to myself as talking about the religion of love, but only as an actual putting it into practice."

"No one who opens the sluices to let a flood of skepticism pour itself over the land must expect to be able to bring it back within its proper bounds. Of those who let themselves get too disheartened to try any longer to discover truth by their own thinking, only a few find a substitute for it in truth taken from others. The mass of people remain skeptical. They lose all feeling for truth, and all sense of need for it as well, finding themselves quite comfortable in a life without thought, driven now here, now there, from one opinion to another."

"Truth has no special time of its own. Its hour is now, always, and indeed then most truly when it seems most unsuitable to actual circumstances."

"Not less strong than the will to truth must be the will to sincerity. Only an age which can show the courage of sincerity can possess truth which works as a spiritual force within it."

"When I look back upon my early days I am stirred by the thought of the number of people whom I have to thank for what they gave me or for what they were to me. At the same time I am haunted by an oppressive consciousness of the little gratitude I really showed them while I was young. How many of them have said farewell to life without my having made clear to them what it meant to me to receive from them so much kindness or so much care! Many a time have I, with a feeling of shame, said quietly to myself over a grave the words which my mouth ought to have spoken to the departed, while he was still in the flesh."

"Developing a true sense of gratitude involves taking absolutely *nothing* for granted, wherever it be, whatever its source. Rather, we always look for the friendly intention behind the deed and learn to appreciate it. Make a point of measuring at its true value every act of kindness you receive from other men. Nothing that may happen to you is purely accidental. Everything can be traced back to a will for good directed in your favor."

"Other demands of gratitude, asked by the thoughtless person, must be refused by the ethical person. I mean the silly and superficial expectations we attach as strings to the good we do. When we have done people a good turn, we expect them to speak well of us. If they don't do it loudly enough, we think they are being ungrateful. When you feel the words 'ingratitude is the thanks you get from the world' forming on the tip of your tongue—stop and listen. Perhaps it is the voice of vanity in your heart. If you can still be honest with yourself, you will often find this to be so. Then tell your heart to be quiet, and revise your notions of what gratitude is entitled to expect. Take warning from the realization that thoughtless people generally complain most about ingratitude. Those who think seriously about the ingratitude they encounter do not find it as easy to be indignant."

"Like all human beings, I am a person who is full of contradictions."

"I listened, in my youth, to conversations between grown-up people through which there breathed a tone of sorrowful regret which oppressed the heart. The speakers looked back at the idealism and capacity for enthusiasm of their youth as something precious to which they ought to have held fast, and yet at the same time they regarded it as almost a law of nature that no one should be able to do so. This woke in me a dread of having ever, even once, to look back on my past with such a feeling; I resolved never to let myself become subject to this tragic domination of mere reason, and what I thus vowed in almost boyish defiance I have tried to carry out."

"As soon as man does not take his existence for granted, but beholds it as something unfathomably mysterious, thought begins."

"To the question whether I am a pessimist or an optimist, I answer that my knowledge is pessimistic, but my willing and hoping are optimistic."

"But granted that we have so trained ourselves that the ugly, vain, and superficial have no part in our expectations of gratitude; granted, too, that we have been so successful in purifying our motives that we really try to do good for its own sake and not in the hope of being appreciated—we shall still be hurt by the prevalence of ingratitude. . . . Disappointment that wounds our soul is a demoralizing thing. . . . All of us find it difficult to hold fast to an optimistic philosophy of life that gives us strength to do good. That is why ingratitude, which is constantly killing our enthusiasm, is one of evil's worst forces."

"The most valuable knowledge we can have is how to deal with disappointments."

"In action lies wisdom and confidence. A man who does not act gets no further than the maxim: Life means conflict and tribulation. But a man who acts can attain the higher wisdom and know that life is conflict and victory. That is why God forces men to labor. That is why he gives them children to bring up. That is why he gives them duties. Through action, they may reach a deeper realization."

"Never say there is nothing beautiful in the world anymore. There is always something to make you wonder in the shape of a tree, the trembling of a leaf."

"The deeper we look into nature the more we recognize that it is full of life, and the more profoundly we know that all life is a secret, and we are all united to all this life."

"All thinking must renounce the attempt to explain the universe. . . . The spirit of the universe is at once destructive and creative—it creates while it destroys, and destroys while it creates . . . and we must inevitably resign ourselves to this."

"As we acquire more knowledge, things do not become more comprehensible but more mysterious."

"Love cannot be put under a system of rules and regulations. It issues absolute commands. Each of us must decide for himself how far he can go towards carrying out the boundless commandment of love without surrendering his own existence and must decide, too, how much of his life and happiness he must sacrifice to the life and happiness of others."

"A man and a woman have not experienced everything together in life unless, looking at each other, they have involuntarily asked the question: What would become of you without me?"

"We must become good plowmen. Hope is the pre-requisite of plowing. What sort of farmer plows the furrow in the autumn but has no hope for the spring? So, too, we accomplish nothing without hope, without a sure inner hope that a new age is about to dawn. Hope is strength. The energy in the world is equal to the hope in it. And even if only a few people share such hopes, a power is created which nothing can hold down—it inevitably spreads to others.

"The second essential of plowing is silence. We must learn that all of our talking and planning is powerless. Modest, quiet work in the kingdom of God is the order of the day.

"The third need when plowing is to work in solitude. We expect all kinds of salvation from meetings, congresses, and organized cooperation. But we deceive ourselves. The most blessed labors can only be accomplished alone, and that is just what we must learn—to work independently. Even if several plowmen plow one field, each follows his own plow. They do not talk to one another; each sees his neighbor and senses the nearness of his fellow worker, all bound together in a common, wordless task."

"We are like waves that do not move individually but rise and fall in rhythm. To share, to rise and fall in rhythm with life around us, is a spiritual necessity."

"There is in each of us the will-to-live, which is based on the mystery of what we call 'taking an interest.' We cannot live alone. Though man is an egoist, he is never completely so. He must always have some interest in life about him. If for no other reason, he must do so in order to make his own life more perfect. Thus it happens that we want to devote ourselves; we want to take our part in perfecting our ideal of progress; we want to give meaning to the life of the world. This is the basis of our striving for harmony with the spiritual element."

"The essential nature of the will-to-live is found in this, that it is determined to live itself out. It bears in itself the impulse to realize itself to the highest perfection."

"Whence the universe came or whither it is bound, or how it happens to be at all, knowledge cannot tell me.

"Only this: that the will-to-live is present everywhere, even as in me."

REVERENCE
FOR LIFE

"Slowly we crept upstream (on one of the long African errands of mercy), laboriously feeling—it was the dry season—for the channels between the sandbanks. Lost in thought I sat on the deck of the barge, struggling to find the elementary and universal conception of the ethical which I had not discovered in any philosophy. Sheet after sheet I covered with disconnected sentences, merely to keep myself concentrated on the problem. Late on the third day, at the very moment when, at sunset, we were making our way through a herd of hippopotamuses, there flashed upon my mind, unforeseen and unsought, the phrase, 'Reverence for Life.' The iron door had yielded: the path in the thicket had become visible. Now I had found my way to the idea in which world-and-life-affirmation and ethics are contained side by side!"

"Life means strength, will, arising from the abyss, dissolving into the abyss again. Life is feeling, experience, suffering. If you study life deeply, looking with perceptive eyes into the vast animated chaos of this creation, its profundity will seize you suddenly with dizziness."

"Reverence for human suffering and human life, for the smallest and most insignificant, must be the inviolable law to rule the world from now on. In so doing, we do not replace old slogans with new ones and imagine that some good may come out of high-sounding speeches and pronouncements. We must recognize that only a deep-seated change of heart, spreading from one man to another, can achieve such a thing in this world."

"How are we to build a new humanity? Only by leading men toward a true, inalienable ethic of our own. . . . Reverence for life comprises the whole ethic of love in its deepest and highest sense. It is the source of constant renewal for the individual and for mankind."

"You walk outside and it is snowing. You carelessly shake the snow from your sleeves. It attracts your attention: a lacy snowflake glistens in your hand. You can't help looking at it. See how it sparkles in a wonderfully intricate pattern. Then it quivers, and the delicate needles of which it consists contract. It melts and lies dead in your hand. It is no more. The snowflake which fluttered down from infinite space upon your hand, where it sparkled and quivered and died—that is yourself. Wherever you see life—that is yourself!"

"In the hope of reaching the moon men fail to see the flowers that blossom at their feet."

"I cannot but have reverence for all that is called life. I cannot avoid compassion for everything that is called life. That is the beginning and foundation of morality."

" 'Reverence for life,' 'surrender of strangeness,' 'the urge to maintain life'—we hear these expressions around us, and they sound cold and shallow. But even if they are modest words they are rich in meaning. A seed is equally commonplace and insignificant, yet within it rests the germ of a lovely flower or a life-giving food. These simple words contain the basic attitude from which all ethical behavior develops, whether the individual is conscious of it or not. Thus the presupposition of morality is to share everything that goes on around us, not only in human life but in the life of all creatures."

"Any religion or philosophy which is not based on a respect for life is not a true religion or philosophy."

"Just as white light consists of colored rays, so Reverence for Life contains all the components of ethics: love, kindliness, sympathy, empathy, peacefulness, power to forgive."

"Nature looks beautiful and marvelous when you view it from the outside. But when you read its pages like a book, it is horrible. And its cruelty is so senseless! The most precious form of life is sacrificed to the lowliest. A child breathes the germs of tuberculosis. He grows and flourishes but is destined to suffering and a premature death because these lowly creatures multiply in his vital organs. How often in Africa have I been overcome with horror when I examined the blood of a patient who was suffering from sleeping sickness. Why did this man, his face contorted in pain, have to sit in front of me, groaning, 'Oh, my head, my head'? Why should he have to suffer night after night and die a wretched death? Because there, under the microscope, were minute, pale corpuscles, one ten-thousandth of a millimeter long—not very many, sometimes such a very few that one had to look for hours to find them at all."

"The fact that in nature one creature may cause pain to another and even deal with it instinctively in the most cruel way, is a harsh mystery that weighs on us as long as we live."

"The world given over to ignorance and egotism is like a valley shrouded in darkness. Only one creature can escape and catch a glimpse of the light: the highest creature, man. His is the privilege of achieving the knowledge of shared experience and compassion, of transcending the ignorance in which the rest of creation pines."

"We, too, are under the painful law of necessity when, to prolong our own existence, we must bring other creatures to a painful end. But we should never cease to consider this as something tragic and incomprehensible."

"The time will come when public opinion will no longer tolerate amusements based on the mistreatment and killing of animals. The time will come, but when? When will we reach the point that hunting, the pleasure in killing animals for sport, will be regarded as a mental aberration? When will all the killing that necessity imposes upon us be undertaken with sorrow?"

"It was quite incomprehensible to me—this was before I began going to school—why in my evening prayers I should pray for human beings only. So when my mother had prayed with me and had kissed me goodnight, I used to add silently a prayer that I had composed myself for all living creatures. It ran thus: 'O heavenly Father, protect and bless all things that have breath; guard them from all evil, and let them sleep in peace.' "

"It is our duty to share and maintain life. Reverence concerning all life is the greatest commandment in its most elementary form. Or expressed in negative terms: 'Thou shalt not kill.' "

"In everything you recognize yourself. The tiny beetle that lies dead in your path—it was a living creature, struggling for existence like yourself, rejoicing in the sun like you, knowing fear and pain like you. And now it is no more than decaying matter—which is what you will be sooner or later, too."

"When I hear a baby's cry of pain change into a normal cry of hunger, to my ears that is the most beautiful music—and there are those who say I have good ears for music."

"Whoever is spared personal pain must feel himself called to help in diminishing the pain of others."

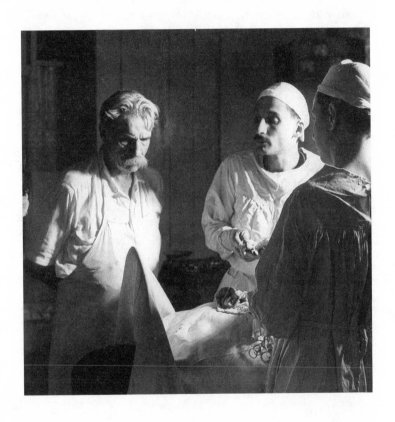

"The fellowship of those who bear the Mark of Pain. Who are the members of this Fellowship? Those who have learnt by experience what physical pain and bodily anguish mean, belong together all the world over; they are united by a secret bond."

"Only at quite rare moments have I felt really glad to be alive. I could not but feel with a sympathy full of regret all the pain that I saw around me, not only that of men but that of the whole creation. From this community of suffering I have never tried to withdraw myself. It seemed to me a matter of course that we should all take our share of the burden of pain which lies upon the world."

"We have invented many things, but we have not mastered the creation of life. We cannot even create an insect."

"A farmer who has mowed down a thousand flowers in his meadow to feed his cows should take care that on the way home he does not, in wanton pastime, switch off the head of a single flower growing at the edge of the road, for in so doing he injures life without being forced to do so by necessity."

"Let a man begin to think about the mystery of his life and the links which connect him with life that fills the world, and he cannot but bring to bear upon his own life and all other life that comes within his reach the principle of reverence for life."

FAITH

"I cannot define what 'faithful' means. The real meaning begins at the point at which verbal explanation is inadequate and ceases to be. Yet we know in our inner heart what it is trying to say. All the good we may recognize or desire is nothing in itself and leads nowhere unless it is strengthened in the thought of faithfulness. It is just like the hardening of metal. No one can explain how it happens. First it is weak and pliable, but then it becomes a hundred times as strong as it was before. Nor can we explain how every human virtue only achieves strength and fulfillment after it has been hardened on the anvil of faithfulness."

"I have the feeling that the Christian theologians are reluctant to come in through the door I have tried to open. I have tried to relate Christianity to the sacredness of all life. It seems to me this is a vital part of Christianity as I understand it. But the Christian theologians, many of them, confine Christianity to the human form of life. It does not seem to me to be correct. It lacks the essential universalization that I associate with Jesus. Why limit reverence for life to the human form?"

"I was asked to preach in a certain parish in the Lower Alsace. On the previous Thursday the whole region, including the parish where I was to preach, had suffered the worst hailstorm to hit our Alsatian land in living memory. On that Saturday night, as I journeyed by train through the area and saw how the fields had been devastated and everything lost, I felt that the sermon I had prepared just wouldn't do. The people would be coming to church expecting to be comforted by the word of God in their misfortune.

"And so I asked myself: What shall I say to them— God sent this calamity to test you or to punish you? I am sure that had I expressed such thoughts then, it would have seemed to me sheer blasphemy. As I mused, I visioned the picture of the Lord at Gethsemane, and preached on the text: 'Lord, not as I will but as thou wilt.' I showed them how we men cannot understand God's ways. But we can understand through Jesus that in all our suffering we still have a Father in heaven. And I could sense that their hearts were calmed.

"I know that you are all as convinced as I that in spite of suffering we need not doubt God's love and faithfulness. We are still heirs of his kingdom and still his children, and so we may rest assured that he will always lift us above misfortune. That is why our Lord says to us: 'Blessed are those who suffer, for they shall be comforted.' "

"The primary insight is man's awareness that his destiny is not synonymous with his daily experiences. You who have been through so much suffering have tasted this inner freedom from outward events. You know there have been times when, according to the rules, you should have been smashed to the ground by what occurred. In such moments you were surprised by yourselves. You had the feeling you were being lifted up inwardly, as though the spiritual were triumphing over the material. You recognized a sort of happiness—if it can be called that—a happiness which would have been hidden by an unbroken succession of good days. You began to understand what the apostle Paul meant when he said, 'Though our outward man perish, yet the inward man is renewed day by day.' The peace of God begins when this fleeting experience can be preserved and turned into a permanent conviction."

"It is harder for us today to feel near to God among the streets and houses of the city than it is for country folk. For them the harvested fields bathed in the autumn mists speak of God and his goodness far more vividly than any human lips."

"To hope, to keep silent, and to work alone—that is what we must learn to do if we really want to labor in the true spirit. But what exactly does it involve, this plowing? The plowman does not pull the plow. He does not push it. He only directs it. This is just how events move in our lives. We can do nothing but guide them straight in the direction which leads to our Lord Jesus Christ, striving toward him, and the furrow will plow itself."

"The paths into which God leads mankind are shrouded in darkness for us. There are only two ground rules. They go together, and each taken by itself is enigmatic. The first is that all sin requires atonement. The second is that all progress demands sacrifice, which has to be paid for by the lives of those chosen to be offered up. We sense this more than we understand it."

"God's love speaks to us in our hearts and tries to work through us in the world. We must listen to it as to a pure and distant melody that comes across the noise of the world's doings. Some say 'When we are grown up, we would rather think of other things.' But the voice of Love with which God speaks to us in the secret places of the heart, speaks to us when we are young so that our youth may be really youth, and that we may become the children of God. Happy are those who listen."

"If you listen you will hear the sound of the kingdom of God in the air as no generation ever could before."

"The ultimate questions of our life transcend knowledge. One riddle after another surrounds us. But the final question of our being has but one concern, and it decides our fate. Again and again we are thrown back to it. What will become of our own will? How does it find itself in the will of God? The highest insight man can attain is the yearning for peace, for the union of his will with an infinite will, his human will with God's will. Such a will does not cut itself off and live in isolation like a puddle that is bound to dry up when the heat of summer comes. No, it is like a mountain stream, relentlessly splashing its way to the river, there to be swept on to the limitless ocean."

THE LIFE OF
THE SOUL

"You know of the disease in Central Africa called sleeping sickness. . . . There also exists a sleeping sickness of the soul. Its most dangerous aspect is that one is unaware of its coming. That is why you have to be careful. As soon as you notice the slightest sign of indifference, the moment you become aware of the loss of a certain seriousness, of longing, of enthusiasm and zest, take it as a warning. You should realize that your soul suffers if you live superficially. People need times in which to concentrate, when they can search their inmost selves. It is tragic that most men have not achieved this feeling of self-awareness. And finally, when they hear the inner voice they do not want to listen anymore. They carry on as before so as not to be constantly reminded of what they have lost. But as for you, resolve to keep a quiet time both in your homes and here within these peaceful walls when the bells ring on Sundays. Then your souls can speak to you without being drowned out by the hustle and bustle of everyday life."

"Don't let your hearts grow numb. Stay alert. It is your soul which matters."

"I do not want to frighten you be telling you about the temptations life will bring. Anyone who is healthy in spirit will overcome them. But there is something I want you to realize. It does not matter so much what you do. What matters is whether your soul is harmed by what you do. If your soul is harmed something irreparable happens, the extent of which you won't realize until it will be too late.

"And others harm their souls even without being exposed to great temptations. They simply let their souls wither. They allow themselves to be dulled by the joys and worries and distractions of life, not realizing that thoughts which earlier meant a great deal to them in their youth turned into meaningless sounds. In the end they have lost all feeling for everything that makes up the inner life."

"So many people gave me something or were something to me without knowing it. . . . I always think that we all live, spiritually, by what others have given us in the significant hours of our life. These significant hours do not announce themselves as coming but arrive unexpected."

"The great enemy of morality has always been indifference. As children, as far as our awareness of things went, we had an elementary capacity for compassion. But our capacity did not develop over the years in proportion to the growth of our understanding. This was uncomfortable and bewildering. We noticed so many people who no longer had compassion or empathy. Then we, too, suppressed our sensitivity so as to be like everyone else. We did not want to be different from them, and we did not know what to do. Thus many people become like houses in which one story after another has been vacated, a lifeless structure in which all windows look empty and strange, deserted."

"The purpose of existence is that we human beings, all nations and the whole of humanity, should constantly progress toward perfection. We must search for these conditions and hold fast to these ideals. If we do this, our finite spirit will be in harmony with the infinite."

"What does the word 'soul' mean? . . . No one can give a definition of the soul. But we know what it feels like. The soul is the sense of something higher than ourselves, something that stirs in us thoughts, hopes, and aspirations which go out to the world of goodness, truth and beauty. The soul is a burning desire to breathe in this world of light and never to lose it—to remain children of light."

"It is reason which helps to get beyond the trivialities of our daily life. We become concerned about all that is happening, with all the questions that beset our times. It makes us participate in this world and feel personally what is happening on earth. . . . Our happiness or unhappiness is not determined by what happens to us in everyday life. However favorable our circumstances, however successful our enterprises, however much envied we are by our fellow men, we still may not be happy. For peace alone is the source of happiness. The more our reasoning throws us into the turmoil of life's problems, the more we yearn for peace. We are led up the mountains until the glaciers begin to glitter before us. Then reasoning bids us climb still higher, still further into the light, still further into peace and quietude."

"The older we grow the more we realize that true power and happiness come to us only from those who spiritually mean something to us. Whether they are near or far, still alive or dead, we need them if we are to find our way through life. The good we bear within us can be turned into life and action only when they are near to us in spirit."

"What tremendous inner power exists in spiritual communion with another man! How pitiable and destitute men are when they are spiritually alone, when they have no one to understand and encourage them. Doubly pitiable if they don't even feel the need for it!"

"For centuries sermons have been preached on the terror of death in order to frighten men into believing in eternal life. And the result? Numbness, numbness. What a strange and fateful phenomenon! In all spheres of life, anything repeated over and over again loses its effect. A ball bounced hundreds and hundreds of times will finally not bounce anymore. The best medicine, taken day in, day out, will no longer be effective. A truth constantly repeated, generation after generation, is eventually disbelieved. That is what has happened all around us. People are no longer moved by fear of death or by the hope of life eternal. All they ask is that death not be mentioned. And thus it seems a conspiracy of silence has descended. We all pretend toward our neighbor that the possibility of his death could never happen."

"We must all become familiar with the thought of death if we want to grow into really good people. We need not think of it every day or every hour. But when the path of life leads us to some vantage point where the scene around us fades away and we contemplate the distant view right to the end, let us not close our eyes. Let us pause for a moment, look at the distant view, and then carry on.

"Thinking about death in this way produces true love for life. When we are familiar with death, we accept each week, each day, as a gift. Only if we are able thus to accept life—bit by bit—does it become precious."

"How can death be overcome? By regarding, in moments of deepest concentration, our lives and those who are part of our lives as though we already had lost them in death, only to receive them back for a little while."

"Only familiarity with the thought of death creates true, inward freedom from material things. The
ambition, greed, and love of power that we keep in
our hearts, that shackle us to this life in chains of
bondage, cannot in the long run deceive the man who
looks death in the face. Rather, by contemplating his
end, he eventually feels purified and delivered from
his baser self, from material things, and from other men,
as well as from fear and hatred of his fellow men."

"The natural contemplation of death can be com-
forting. Have you ever considered how dreadful it would
be if our lives had no appointed end but went on
forever? . . . Can you imagine that as far as the eye can
see into the future we should remain enmeshed in the
desires and troubles of this life and that all the ensuing
envy, hatred, and malice, our own and other people's,
should continue to pile up undiminished?"

"You may think it strange that I have spoken so much about death and not a word about immortality, the word one generally uses to dispel one's fears. Perhaps one has talked too much and too superficially about immortality, in order to comfort people in the face of death. Hence the word has been depreciated. Immortality believed in for the sake of comfort is not genuine immortality. The impression it makes on us is as fleeting as a picture painted on a wall in watercolors—the next shower of rain will wash it away. It is imposed on people from the outside. They soon forget about it, preferring to stifle their fear of death by refusing to think about it.

"But the man who dares to live his life with death before his eyes, the man who receives life back bit by bit and lives as though it did not belong to him by right but has been bestowed on him as a gift, the man who has such freedom and peace of mind that he has overcome death in his thoughts—such a man believes in eternal life because it is already his, it is a present experience, and he already benefits from its peace and joy."

"No one has ever come back from the other world. I can't console you, but one thing I can tell you, as long as my ideals are alive I will be alive."

THE MUSICIAN AS ARTIST

"Joy, sorrow, tears, lamentations, laughter—to all these music gives voice, but in such a way that we are transported from the world of unrest to the world of peace, and see reality in a new way, as if we were sitting by a mountain lake and contemplating hills and woods and clouds in the tranquil and fathomless water."

"The work and the worry that fell to my lot through the practical interest I took in organ building, made me sometimes wish that I had never troubled myself about it, but if I do not give it up, the reason is that the struggle for the good organ is to me a part of the struggle for truth."

"An organ is like a cow; one does not look at its horns so much as at its milk."

"To be artistically beautiful and strong is only to have a figure with a perfect play of muscles. So in time we shall desert the modern organ inflated by wind pressure, seek the full, rich, and beautiful organ only through the collaboration of the normal, differentiated, and artistically toned stops, and give up trying to assemble a full organ by craftiness. Craftiness does not belong with art, for art is truth."

"I had just ended a Bach fugue on a wonderful old Silbermann organ, and was still completely captivated by the magic tone of the old mixtures, when someone next to me, who had his modern organ for two years, remarked, 'You know, it must be disagreeable to play on an organ that does not have a single tilting tablet.' In his irritation over the old drawstops he had not heard the organ."

"The test of every organ, the best and only test, is Bach's organ music. Let one apply this test artistically to organ building, instead of trying to imagine how Bach would throw his peruke in the air for joy over our pistons, and then after catching it again, set off to find out from one of our modern organ virtuosi how on the modern organ one can bring everything out of his music."

"Bach was a poet; and this poet was at the same time a painter. This is not at all a paradox. We have the habit of classifying an artist according to the means he uses to interpret his inner life; a musician if he uses sounds, a painter if he uses colors, a poet if he uses words. But we must admit that these categories, established by external criteria, are very arbitrary. The soul of an artist is a complex whole, in which mingle in proportions infinitely variable the gifts of the poet, the painter, the musician."

"Descriptive music is, then, legitimate; since painting and poetry are like the unconscious elements without which the language of sounds could not be conceived. There is a painter in every musician. Listen to him, and this second nature will immediately appear to you."

"Let us watch Bach at his work. However bad the text, he is satisfied with it if it contains a picture. When he discovers a pictorial idea it takes the place of the whole text; he seizes on it even at the risk of going contrary to the dominant idea of the text. . . . Nature itself he perceives, so to speak, in a pictorial fashion."

"Beethoven and Wagner poetize in music, Bach paints. And Bach is a dramatist, but just in the sense that the painter is. He does not paint successive events, but seizes upon the pregnant moment that contains the whole event for him, and depicts this in music."

"The musical language of Bach is the most elaborate and most precise in existence. It has, after a fashion, its roots and derivations like any other language."

"Music is an act of worship with Bach. His artistic activity and his personality are both based on his piety. . . . For him, art was religion, and so had no concern with the world or with worldly success. It was an end in itself. Bach includes religion in the definition of art in general. All great art, even secular, is in itself religious in his eyes; for him the tones do not perish, but ascend to God like praise too deep for utterance."

CIVILIZATION
AND PEACE

"The ideal of civilized man is none other than that of a man who in every relation of life preserves true human nature. To be civilized men means for us approximately this: that in spite of the conditions of modern civilization we remain human."

"We live in a dark and frightening age. One reason for this is the part played by the ideology of inhumanity in our time."

"The awareness that we are all human beings together has become lost in war and politics. We have reached the point of regarding each other only as members of a people either allied with us or against us and our approach: prejudice, sympathy, or antipathy are all conditioned by that. Now we must rediscover the fact that we—all together—are human beings, and that we must strive to concede to each other what moral capacity we have."

"Man can no longer live for himself alone. We must realize that all life is valuable and that we are united to all life. From this knowledge comes our spiritual relationship with the universe."

"The only way out of today's misery is for people to become worthy of each other's trust."

"Only when the human spirit grows powerful within us and guides us back to a civilization based on humanitarian ideal; only *then* will it act, through our intermediacy, upon those other peoples. All men . . . are endowed with the faculty of compassion, and for this reason can develop the humanitarian spirit. There is inflammable matter within them: let there come a spark, and it will burst into flame."

"Because I have confidence in the power of Truth and of the spirit, I believe in the future of mankind."

"When we observe contemporary society one thing strikes us. We debate but make no progress. Why? Because as peoples we do not yet trust each other."

"We live in a time when the good faith of peoples is doubted more than ever before. Expressions throwing doubt on the trustworthiness of each other are bandied back and forth. They are based on what happened in the First World War when the nations experienced dishonesty, injustice, and inhumanity from one another. How can a new trust come about? And yet, it must.

"We cannot continue in this paralyzing mistrust. If we want to work our way out of the desperate situation in which we find ourselves, another spirit must enter into the people. It can only come if the awareness of its *necessity* suffices to give us strength to believe in its coming."

"The only possible way out of the present chaos is for us to adopt a world-view which will bring us once more under that control of the ideals of true civilization which are contained in it."

"The organized political, social, and religious associations of our time are at work to induce individual man not to arrive at his convictions by his own thinking but to take as his own such convictions as they keep ready-made for him. Any man who thinks for himself and at the same time is spiritually free is to the associations something inconvenient and even uncanny. He does not offer sufficient guarantee that he will merge himself in their organization in the way they wish. All corporate bodies look today for their strength not so much to the spiritual worth of the ideas they represent and to that of the people who belong to them, as to the attainment of the highest possible degree of unity and exclusiveness. It is here that they expect to find their strongest power for offense and defense."

"The history of our time is characterized by a lack of reason which has no parallel in the past. Future historians will one day analyze this history in detail, and test by means of it their learning and their freedom from prejudice. But for all future times there will be, as there is for today, only one explanation, viz., that we sought to live and to carry on with a civilization which has no ethical principle behind it."

"Ethics are responsibility without limit towards all that lives."

"I am worried about present-day journalism. The emphasis on negative happenings is much too strong. Not infrequently, news about events marking great progress is overlooked or minimized. It tends to make for a negative and discouraging atmosphere. There is a danger that people may lose faith in the forward direction of humanity if they feel that very little happens to support that faith. And real progress is related to the belief that it is possible."

"Another hindrance to civilization to-day is the over-organization of our public life.

"While it is certain that a properly ordered environment is the condition and, at the same time, the result of civilization, it is also undeniable that, after a certain point has been reached, external organization is developed at the expense of the spiritual life. Personality and ideas are often subordinated to institutions, when it is really these which ought to influence the latter and keep them inwardly alive."

"Man has lost the capacity to foresee and forestall. He will end by destroying the earth."

"What we seem to forget is that, yes, the sun will continue to rise and set and the moon will continue to move across the skies, but mankind can create a situation in which the sun and moon can look down upon an earth that has been stripped of all life."

"Those who conduct an atomic war for freedom will die, or end their lives miserably. Instead of freedom they will find destruction. Radioactive clouds resulting from a war between East and West would imperil humanity everywhere. There would be no need to use up the remaining stock of atom and H-bombs. An atomic war is therefore the most senseless and lunatic act that could ever take place. At all costs it must be prevented."

"In an atomic war there would be neither conqueror nor vanquished. During such a bombardment both sides would suffer the same fate. A continuous destruction would take place and no armistice nor peace proposals would bring it to an end."

"At this stage we have the choice of two risks: the one lies in continuing the mad atomic-arms race with its danger of an unavoidable atomic war in the near future; the other in the renunciation of nuclear weapons, and in the hope that the United States and the Soviet Union, and the peoples associated with them, will manage to live in peace. The first holds no hope of a prosperous future; the second does. We must risk the second."

"At the present time when violence, clothed in life, dominates the world more cruelly than it ever has before, I still remain convinced that truth, love, peaceableness, meekness, and kindness are the violence which can master all other violence."

"In the hearts of people today there is a deep longing for peace. When the true spirit of peace is thoroughly dominant, it becomes an inner experience with unlimited possibilities. It is only when this really happens, that the spirit of peace awakens and takes possession of men's hearts, that humanity can be saved from perishing."

"Is the human spirit able to achieve those things which, in our distress, we must expect of it?

"We must not underestimate its strength. Through human history this strength has made itself manifest. It is to the strength of the human mind that we owe the humanitarianism that is at the origin of a progress towards a higher way of life. When we are animated by humanitarianism we are faithful to ourselves and capable of creation."

The Problem of Peace
in the World of Today

. . . We have not taken proper notice of history; and, in consequence, we no longer know what is just—or what is useful. . . . The most flagrant violation of the rights of history—and, above all, of the rights of man— occurs when a people is deprived of the right to the land on which it lives and has to move elsewhere. At the end of the second world war the victorious powers decided to impose this fate upon hundreds of thousands of people, and to impose [it] in the cruelest conditions; in this they showed how little they understood their task, and how unfitted they were to carry out a reorganization which would be reasonably equitable and might guarantee a more prosperous future. . . .

And now—what exactly is this problem of peace in the modern world? Its conditions are quite new—as different from those of former times as is the war which we seek to avert. Modern warfare is fought with weapons which are incomparably more destructive than those of the past. War is, in fact, a greater evil than ever before. It was once possible to regard it as an evil to which we could resign ourselves, because it was the servant of progress—and was even essential to it. It could be argued in those days that, thanks to war, those nations which were strongest got the better of their weaker neighbors and thus determined the march of history. . . .

It is worth remembering that for the generation which

grew up before 1914, the enormous increase in the destructive power of modern armament was regarded as advantageous to humanity. It was argued that the outcome of any future conflict would be settled much more quickly than in previous ages, and that any such wars would therefore be very brief.

It was also thought that the harm done by any future conflict would be relatively slight, since a new element of humanity was being introduced into the rules of war. This arose from the obligations established by the Geneva Convention of 1864 as a result of the efforts of the Red Cross. The nations had entered into a mutual agreement to look after each other's wounded, to ensure that prisoners of war were treated humanely, and to see that the civil populations were disturbed as little as possible. This convention did, in point of fact, have substantial results, and hundreds of thousands of men, civilians and combatants alike, have profited by it for the last ninety years. But these advantages are trifling when set beside the immeasurable harm which has been inflicted by modern methods of death and destruction. There cannot, at the present time, be any question of "humanizing" war. . . .

Now that we know how terrible an evil war is in our time, we should neglect nothing that may prevent its recurrence. Above all, this decision must be based on ethical values: during the last two wars we were guilty of atrocious acts of inhumanity. In any future war, we shall do yet more terrible things. This must not be.

Let us be brave and look the facts in the face. Man has become a superman. He is a superman not only because he has at his command innate physical forces, but because, thanks to science and to technical advancement, he now controls the latent forces of nature and can bring them, if he wishes, into play. When quite on his own he could only kill at a distance by calling upon the personal strength which enabled him to draw his bow; and this strength he communicated to the arrow by suddenly unleashing his bow. Superman, on the other hand, has contrived to unleash something quite different: the energy released by the deflagration of a particular mixture of chemicals. This allows him to use a vastly more formidable projectile, and he can send it a great deal farther.

But this superman suffers from a fatal imperfection of mind. He has not raised himself to that superhuman level of reason which should correspond to the possession of superhuman strength. . . .

Today, once again, we live in a period that is marked by the absence of peace; today, once again, nations feel themselves menaced by other nations; today, once again, we must concede to each the right to defend himself with the terrible weapons which are now at our disposal. . . .

I believe that I have here given voice to the thoughts and hopes of millions of human beings in our part of the world who live in fear of a future war. May my words be understood in their true sense, if they happen to reach those on the far side of the barrier who are haunted by this same fear.

May those who have in their hands the fate of the nations take care to avoid whatever may worsen our situation and make it more dangerous. And may they take to heart the words of the Apostle Paul: "If it be possible, as much as lieth in you, live peaceably with all men." His words are valid not only for individuals, but for whole nations as well. May the nations, in their efforts to keep peace in being, go to the farthest limits of possibility, so that the spirit of man shall be given time to develop and grow strong—and time to act.

Excerpt from the address delivered by Dr. Schweitzer in Oslo, in November 1954, when he accepted the Nobel Peace Prize awarded him in 1952.

CHRONOLOGY

1875

January 14   Born at Kaysersberg, Haute Alsace. During this year his father became pastor at Günsbach, in the Munster Valley, Haute Alsace.

1893

June 18   Passed his matriculation examination for the university at the Mulhouse Gymnasium.

October   First sojourn in Paris. Studied the organ under Widor.

November   Began study at the University of Strasbourg in theology, philosophy, and musical theory, living in the Theological Seminary of St. Thomas. While at the university wrote his first book, a small brochure in French upon the life and activity of Eugene Munch, his former organ teacher at Mulhouse, who died of typhoid fever at the beginning of Schweitzer's career.

1894

April–April, 1895   Military service in infantry regiment 143.

1897

Autumn   Wrote thesis required of all candidates for the first examination in theology upon the topic prescribed by the faculty: "The Idea of the Last Supper in Daniel Scheleiermacher, Compared with the Ideas of Luther, Zwingli, and Calvin."

1898

May 6   Passed his first theological examination before the faculty.

Summer   Continued to study philosophy at the University of Strasbourg under Ziegler and Windelband. At the end of summer he proposed to Professor Ziegler as the theme of his doctoral thesis a study of Kant's philosophy of religion in relation to the different stages of what seemed to him its constant evolution.

**Autumn–Spring
1899**   Studied at the Sorbonne in Paris; devoted himself to his organ studies under Widor.

1899

April–July	At Berlin for study of philosophy and organ.
End of July	Received Ph.D. at Strasbourg after examination in philosophy.
December	Appointed Lehr-Vicar at St. Nicholas in Strasbourg, in compliance with the rules requiring a student to serve in a church for a period between his first and second theological examinations.
End of December	*The Religious Philosophy of Kant from the "Critique of Pure Reason" to "Religion Within the Bounds of Mere Reason"* published by J.C.B. Mohr at Tübingen.

1900

July 15	Passed second theological examination before a commission of learned pastors.
July 21	Obtained the degree of licentiate in theology with his study of the Last Supper.
September 23	Ordained at St. Nicholas as a regular curate.

1901

May 1— **September 30**	Received provisional appointment as Principal of the Protestant Theological Seminary. *The Mystery of the Kingdom of God* published by Mohr at Tübingen.

1903

October 1	Received permanent appointment as Principal of the Protestant Theological Seminary. Moved from the city to his official quarters on the Embankment of St. Thomas.

1905

January 14	Thirtieth birthday. Decided to devote the rest of his life to the natives of equatorial Africa as a doctor of medicine. *J.S. Bach* published by Costallat in Paris.
October 13	Made known his decision to serve as a missionary doctor, and entered into discussion with Paris Missionary Society.
1906	Resigned from the directorship of the Theological Seminary. Began study as a medical student at the University of Strasbourg. *The Quest of the Histori-*

cal Jesus published by Mohr at Tübingen, and the treatise *German and French Organ-Building and Organ-Playing* published by Breitkopf and Hartel in Leipzig.

1909

May — Gave address to organ section of Third Congress, International Society of Music, in Vienna, and played a major role in formulating the International Regulations for Organ Building recommended by the organ section.

1911 — *Paul and His Interpreters* published by Mohr at Tübingen.

Autumn — Played the organ for Widor's Second Symphony for Organ and Orchestra at the Festival of French Music at Munich.

Autumn–December — Passed his examination in medicine at Strasbourg, during a period of terrible exhaustion.

1912

Spring — Resigned his posts as a teacher in the university and as a preacher at St. Nicholas.

June 18 — Married Helene Bresslau, daughter of the Strasbourg historian. Afterwards retired to his father's house in Gunsbach to work on the second edition of *Paul and His Interpreters*, assisted by his wife.

1913

February — Having completed his year of internship, and having finished his thesis, received the degree of doctor of medicine.

March 26 — Embarked at Bordeaux for Africa, where he established a hospital on the grounds of the Lambaréné station of the Paris Missionary Society. *The Psychiatrical Study of Jesus* and the second edition of *Paul and His Interpreters* published by Mohr at Tübingen.

August–November 1914 — Interned with his wife at Lambaréné as an enemy alien. Began his work on *The Philosophy of Civilization*.

1915

September   While on a 200–kilometer journey up the Ogowe River to N'Gomo, suddenly the words "Reverence for Life" came to him as the elementary and universal conception of ethics for which he had been searching. Upon this principle his whole philosophy of civilization was subsequently based.

1917

September   Transferred with his wife to France as a civil intern.

1918

Spring   Transferred to St. Remy de Provence. Served as a doctor during the daytime and worked on his philosophy during the evenings.

End of July   Returned to Alsace in an exchange of prisoners.

1919   Accepted a post as preacher at St. Nicholas, and also a post as physician in the City Hospital of Strasbourg.

January 14   Daughter born on his birthday.

1920

Spring   Delivered a course of lectures at Uppsala in Sweden, using as his subject the problem of world-and-life-affirmation and ethics in philosophy and world-religions. Gave a series of organ concerts and lectures in Sweden to pay off the debts he had incurred for the hospital.

Honorary doctorate from Theological faculty in Zurich. *On The Edge of the Primeval Forest* published at Uppsala.

1921

April   Gave up both positions at Strasbourg and returned to Günsbach, where he was appointed vicar to his father, in order to work quietly on his *Philosophy of Civilization*.

1923

Spring   *The Philosophy of Civilization* published by C.H. Beck in Munich and Paul Haupt in Berne in two volumes, *The Decay and Restoration of Civilization* and *Civilization and Ethics*. Also in the same year Allen and Unwin published in London *Christianity and the World-Religions*.

1924
February

Wrote *Memoirs of Childhood and Youth*, published by Allen and Unwin in London the same year.

February 14

Left Strasbourg for Africa, leaving his wife behind in Europe because of her poor health.

April 19

Began second sojourn in Africa, which lasted until July 21, 1927. Compelled to reconstruct the hospital, which had fallen into ruin, and later to transfer it to a new and roomier site at Adolinanongo, where the new buildings were constructed of hardwood and corrugated iron. During this period of rebuilding Schweitzer had to abandon all literary work. In the morning he worked as a doctor, in the afternoon as a laborer. The number of patients constantly increased and he was obliged to send to Europe for two more doctors and two more nurses. He was able, however, to keep up his regular practice on his piano with organ pedals. Reports of his work in Africa were sent to Europe in the form of letters to friends and supporters and published in three small volumes by Beck in Munich and Haupt in Berne.

1925

Received honorary degree of Doctor of Philosophy from the University of Prague in absentia.

1927
July

Returned to Europe. Lectures and concert tours in Sweden, Denmark, Holland, Germany, Switzerland, England, and Czechoslovakia. During this period devoted all his spare time to his book on *The Mysticism of Paul the Apostle*. The book was finished on the boat that took him back to Africa in December 1929.

1928
August 28

Received Goethe Prize from the City of Frankfurt, delivering an address there on his indebtedness to Goethe.

1929
December 26

Began third sojourn in Africa, which ended January 7, 1932. During this period he wrote his autobiography, *Out of My Life and Thought*; it was published by Felix Meiner in Leipzig in 1931.

1931

Received honorary degrees of Doctor of Divinity and Doctor of Music from the University of Edinburgh.

1932

Received honorary degrees of Doctor of Philosophy from Oxford University and Doctor of Laws from St. Andrews University.

February

Returned to Europe. Lectures and concerts in Holland, England, Sweden, German, and Switzerland. Worked on the third volume of *The Philosophy of Civilization*.

1933
April 21

Began fourth sojourn in Africa, which lasted until January 11, 1934. All of his leisure time was given to the third volume of his philosophy.

1934
Autumn

Hibbert Lectures at Manchester College, Oxford, under the subject "Religion in Modern Civilization."

November

Gifford Lectures at Edinburgh, in which he endeavored to trace the progress of human thought from the great thinkers of India, China, Greece, and Persia. The chapter on the evolution of Indian thought grew to such an extent that he decided to publish it as a separate book, *Indian Thought and Its Development*, published by Beck in Munich in 1934.

1935
February 26

Began fifth sojourn to Africa, which ended August 22, 1935.

November

Second course of Gifford Lectures. Lectures and concerts in England.

1936

Worked on his philosophy, and in October recorded organ music for Columbia Records in London upon the organ of St. Aurelia's at Strasbourg.

1937

February 18   Began sixth sojourn to Africa, which ended on January 10, 1939. Schweitzer carried with him the manuscript for his philosophy, believing that now at last he would be able to finish it, but the increasing responsibilities of the hospital left him little time.

1938   Wrote *From My African Notebook*, a little volume of anecdotes upon the ideas and the lives of the natives, published by Meiner in Leipzig that same year.

1939

January 10   Left for Europe with the hope of completing his third volume.

February   Arrived in Europe, only to decide that war could not be avoided, and might break out at any moment. Returned immediately to Africa.

March 3   Began seventh sojourn in Africa, which ended in October 1948. During the first two years of the war he was able to work continuously on his writing; but afterwards the scarcity of hospital personnel made it necessary for him to devote himself almost exclusively to the care of the sick and to other hospital duties. Toward the end of 1945 he wrote an account of the war years at Lambaréné, under the title *Lambaréné 1939–1945*.

1948

September   Returned to Europe, visiting his wife at Königsfeld in the Black Forest, seeing his four grandchildren for the first time in Switzerland—but spending most of his time as usual at his home in Günsbach. Worked on a theological book and on the third volume of his *Philosophy of Civilization*.

1949

June 28   Arrived in New York for his first visit to America. Received honorary degree of Doctor of Laws from the University of Chicago in the Rockefeller Memorial Chapel. Visited New York, Boston, and a few other cities, after which he returned to his home in Alsace.

October	Began eighth sojourn in Africa, which ended in May 1951. Intensified his work for those afflicted with leprosy, using the discoveries of American medical science.
1950	Made a Chevalier of the Legion of Honor.

1951

May–December	In Europe. On September 15, 1951, received the 10,000-mark prize given by the West German Association of Book Publishers and Book Sellers at Frankfurt, Germany, in recognition of his efforts in promoting world peace. Turned the money over to German refugees and destitute writers.
December 3	Elected a member of the French Academy of Moral and Political Sciences.
December	Began ninth sojourn in Africa, which ended in July 1952.

1952

February 27	Awarded the Prince Charles Medal by King Gustav Adolf for his great humanitarian achievements.
July–November	In Europe.
November	Began tenth sojourn in Africa, which ended in May 1954. Began to construct, in memory of his father and mother, a new village for Africans suffering from leprosy.

1953

October 30	The 1952 Nobel Peace Prize was awarded to Schweitzer in absentia, and was accepted in his name by the French ambassador to Norway. Schweitzer announced that the money (roughly $36,000) would be used toward the expenses of constructing his leprosy hospital.

1954

May 12	Was made a foreign honorary member of the American Academy of Arts and Sciences.

1954

May–December	In Europe. At Oslo on November 4, 1954, to deliver in the presence of King Gustav Adolf the long-awaited Nobel Peace Prize address on "The Problem of Peace in the World of Today."

December	Began eleventh sojourn in Africa, which ended in May 1955. Finished most of the work for the new leprosy hospital.

1955

January 14	Celebrated his eightieth birthday at Lambaréné. On that same day received the Gold Medal of the City of Paris.
May–December	In Europe. On October 19, 1955, was made an honorary member of the British Order of Merit by Queen Elizabeth. On October 22, received an honorary degree of Doctor of Laws from the University of Cambridge. On November 11, President Heuss of the West German Republic awarded Schweitzer the order *Pour le Merite*.
December	Returned to Africa for his twelfth sojourn.

1956

January 14	Celebrated his eighty-first birthday in Lambaréné.

1957

May 30	Death of Helene Schweitzer in Switzerland.
August 23	Arrived in Europe.
December 4	Embarked from Bordeaux for Africa, arriving at his hospital in Lambaréné on Christmas Day. He carried with him the ashes of his wife.

1958

January 14	Spent his eighty-third birthday at his hospital post.
	Broadcast "Peace or Atomic War?" from Oslo.

1963

April	Received an address of felicitation on the jubilee of Lambaréné from supporters in twenty-eight countries.

1965

September 4	Died at Lambaréné and was buried there.

SOURCES

The quotations in this book were selected from the speeches, sermons, and published works of Albert Schweitzer, and from passages in works written about him. Unless otherwise indicated, all publications are by Dr. Schweitzer. (Refer to the abbreviated titles given in parentheses after each source in order to identify individual quotations on the page-by-page reference list that follows.)

Address given at the Schweitzer Gymnasium, 1959. (Gymnasium)

The Animal World of Albert Schweitzer, translated by Charles R. Joy. Boston: Beacon Press, 1950. (Animal World)

Animals, Nature, and Albert Schweitzer, by Ann Cottrell Free. Great Barrington, Massachusetts: The Albert Schweitzer Center, 1982. (Nature)

The Courier. New York: publication of The Albert Schweitzer Fellowship, Summer 1982. (Courier)

"A Declaration of Conscience," *Saturday Review,* May 18, 1957. (Declaration)

Dr. Schweitzer of Lambaréné, by Norman Cousins. New York: Harper & Row, 1960. (Lambaréné)

"The Ethics of Reverence for Life," in *Christendom,* Vol. 1, No. 2, Winter 1936. (Ethics)

For All That Lives, by Ann Atwood and Erica Anderson. New York: Charles Scribner's Sons, 1975. (For All)

Interview with the Governor of Gabon, 1958. (Gabon)

J. S. Bach, Volumes I & II. New York: The Macmillan Company, 1964. (J. S. Bach)

Memoirs of Childhood and Youth. New York: The Macmillan Company, 1963. (Memoirs)

Music in the Life of Albert Schweitzer, by Charles R. Joy. New York: Harper & Brothers, 1951. (Music)

On the Edge of the Primeval Forest. New York: The Macmillan Company, 1948. (Primeval)

Out of My Life and Thought. New York: Henry Holt, 1933. (Life and Thought)

Peace or Atomic War? New York: Henry Holt & Co., 1958. (Peace)
The Philosophy of Civilization. New York: The Macmillan Company,
1932. (Philosophy)
The Problem of Peace in the World of Today, Nobel Peace Prize accep-
tance speech. New York: Harper & Brothers, 1954. (Problem)
Prophet in the Wilderness, by Hermann Hagedorn. New York: The
Macmillan Company, 1947. (Prophet)
Reverence for Life. New York: Harper & Row, 1966. (Reverence)
Reverence Newsletter, No. 4. Great Barrington, Massachusetts: publica-
tion of The Albert Schweitzer Center. (Newsletter)
Saturday Review Treasury, by John Haverstick and the editors of *Sat rday
Review.* New York: Simon & Schuster, 1957. (Saturday Review)
The Schweitzer Album, by Erica Anderson. New York: Harper & Row,
1965. (Album)
The Teaching of Reverence for Life. New York: Holt, Rinehart & Winston,
1965. (Teaching)
The World of Albert Schweitzer, by Erica Anderson and E. Exman.
New York: Harper & Brothers, 1955. (World)

p. 15: Album, Memoirs; p. 16: Lambaréné, Lambaréné, Lambaréné;
p. 17: Memoirs, Memoirs, World; p. 19: Life and Thought,
Primeval, Life and Thought; p. 20: Memoirs, Reverence; p. 21:
Reverence, Album; p. 22: Memoirs, Teaching; p. 24: Life and
Thought, Reverence, Memoirs; p. 25: Reverence, For All, For All;
p. 26: For All, Album, Animal World, Reverence; p. 27: Reverence,
Album; p. 29: Ethics, For All, For All; p. 33: Life and Thought,
Reverence; p. 35: Reverence, Reverence; p. 36: Reverence, Gabon,
Reverence; p. 37: Reverence, Nature, Teaching; p. 39: Reverence;
p. 40: For All, Reverence, For All; p. 41: Teaching, Memoirs,
Reverence; p. 42: Reverence, Album, Saturday Review; p. 44:
Primeval, World, For All; p. 45: For All, For All; p. 49: Rev-
erence, Lambaréné; p. 50: Reverence; p. 51: Reverence, Reverence;
p. 53: Reverence, Reverence; p. 54: Prophet, Reverence; p. 54–55:
Reverence; p. 59: Reverence; p 60: Reverence, Reverence; p. 61:
Memoirs, Reverence; p. 63: Reverence, Reverence; p. 65: Rev-
erence, Reverence; p. 66: Reverence, Reverence; p. 67: Reverence,
Reverence; p. 68: Reverence, Reverence; p. 69: Reverence,
Newsletter; p. 73: World, Life and Thought, World; p. 74: Music,
Music, Music; p. 75: Music, Music, Music; p. 77: J. S. Bach,
Music, J. S. Bach; p. 81: Philosophy, Teaching, Peace; p. 83: Nature,
World, Problem, Life and Thought; p, 84: Gymnasium, Peace,

Life and Thought; p. 85: Life and Thought, Philosophy; p. 87: Philosophy, Lambaréné, Philosophy; p. 88: Nature, Declaration, Peace; p. 89: Peace, Peace, Memoirs; p. 91: Courier, Problem.

The photographs incorporated in this book are from the following sources:

p. 2: Dr. Schweitzer; by Clara Urquhart.

p. 12: Schweitzer's study at Günsbach, France; by Erica Anderson, courtesy Albert Schweitzer Center.

p. 18: Signpost in the Schweitzer Village, Lambaréné, Africa; by Norman Cousins.

p. 23: Schweitzer as a young man, Günsbach; courtesy Albert Schweitzer Center.

p. 28: On a hill near Günsbach; by Erica Anderson, courtesy Albert Schweitzer Center.

p. 30: Dr. Margaret van der Kreek cradles a baby in a hat, Lambaréné; by Norman Cousins.

p. 34: African landscape; by Clara Urquhart.

p. 38: Feeding an antelope, Lambaréné; by Erica Anderson, courtesy Albert Schweitzer Center.

p. 43: In the operating room at Lambaréné; by Erica Anderson, courtesty Albert Schweitzer Center.

p. 46: In a church in Günsbach; by Erica Anderson, courtesy Albert Schweitzer Center.

p. 52: On the path through the jungle from the leper ward to the hospital; by Erica Anderson, courtesy Albert Schweitzer Center.

p. 56: By Clara Urquhart.

p. 62: In the Schweitzer Village; by Clara Urquhart.

p. 64: In a *pirogue;* by Erica Anderson, courtesy Albert Schweitzer Center.

p. 70: Marking a music manuscript; by Erica Anderson, courtesy Albert Schweitzer Center.

p. 76: By Erica Anderson, courtesy Albert Schweitzer Center.

p. 78: On the porch, Lambaréné; by Erica Anderson, courtesy Albert Schweitzer Center.

p. 82: Scene at Lambaréné, at Christmas; by Erica Anderson, courtesy Norman Cousins.

p. 86: By Norman Cousins.

p. 90: Schweitzer and others from the Lambaréné clinic seeing a nurse off on her sabbatical in Europe; by Norman Cousins.

p. 92: By Erica Anderson, courtesy Albert Schweitzer Center.

p. 106: By Clara Urquhart.

THE ACCLAIMED NEWMARKET *WORDS OF* SERIES

The Words of Peace
Selections from the Speeches of the Winners of the Nobel Peace Prize
Edited by Professor Irwin Abrams. Foreword by President Jimmy Carter.
A new compendium of excerpts from the award winners' acceptance speeches from 1901 to 1990, including the Dalai Lama, Mother Teresa, Lech Walesa, Martin Luther King, Jr., and Elie Wiesel. Themes are: Peace, Human Rights, Violence and Nonviolence, the Bonds of Humanity, Faith and Hope, plus much more. 144 pages. 4" x 6". ISBN 1-55704-250-0, $6.95 pocket paperback.
5 1/4" x 8". ISBN 1-55704-060-5, $14.95 hardcover.

The Words of Desmond Tutu
Selected and introduced by Naomi Tutu
Nearly 100 memorable quotations from the addresses, sermons, and writings of South Africa's Nobel Prize-winning Archbishop. Topics include: Faith and Responsibility, Apartheid, Family, Violence and Nonviolence, The Community—Black and White, and Toward a New South Africa.
10 photos; chronology; text of acceptance speech for the Nobel Peace Prize, 1984. 112 pages.
5 1/4" x 8". ISBN 1-55704-038-9, $12.95 hardcover. ISBN 1-55704-215-2, $9.95 paperback.

The Words of Gandhi
Selected and introduced by Richard Attenborough
Over 150 selections from the letters, speeches, and writings collected in five sections—Daily Life, Cooperation, Nonviolence, Faith, and Peace.
21 photos; glossary. 112 pages. 5 1/4" x 8". ISBN 0-937858-14-5, $10.95 hardcover.

The Words of Harry S Truman
Selected and introduced by Robert J. Donovan
This entirely new volume of quotations from Truman's speeches and writings gives the essence of his views on politics, leadership, civil rights, war and peace, and on "giving 'em hell."
15 photos; chronology. 112 pages. 5 1/4" x 8". ISBN: 1-55704-283-7. $9.95 paperback.

The Words of Martin Luther King, Jr.
Selected and introduced by Coretta Scott King
Over 120 quotations and excerpts from the great civil rights leader's speeches, sermons, and writings on: The Community of Man, Racism, Civil Rights, Justice and Freedom, Faith and Religion, Nonviolence, and Peace. 16 photos; chronology; text of presidential proclamation of King holiday.
128 pages. 5 1/4" x 8". ISBN 0-937858-28-5, $14.95, hardcover. ISBN 0-937858-79-X, $9.95 paperback. 4" x 6". ISBN 1-55704-151-2, $5.95 pocket paperback.

The Words of Albert Schweitzer
Selected and introduced by Norman Cousins
An inspiring collection focusing on: Knowledge and Discovery, Reverence for Life, Faith, The Life of the Soul, The Musician as Artist, and Civilization and Peace.
22 photos; chronology. 112 pages. 5 1/4" x 8". ISBN 0-937858-41-2, $14.95 hardcover.

More Inspirational Biography
Gandhi: A Pictorial Biography
Text by Gerald Gold, Photo Selection and Afterword by Richard Attenborough
The important personal, political and spiritual periods of Gandhi's life. "First Rate."—*LA Times*.
150 photos; bibliography; map; index. 192 pages. 7 1/4" x 9". ISBN 0-937858-20-X, $9.95 paperback

Newmarket Press books are available from your local bookseller or from Newmarket Press, 18 East 48th Street, New York, NY 10017. (212) 832-3575. Catalogs are available on request. Please add $3.00 per book for postage and handling, plus $1.00 for each additional item ordered. (New York residents, please add applicable state and local sales tax.) Please allow 4-6 weeks for delivery. Prices and availability are subject to change. For information on quantity order discounts, please contact the Newmarket Special Sales Department.